W9-CLR-814

SOFTBALL'S POWER OFFENSE

Susan Craig
Ken Johnson

COACHES
CHOICE

ISBN: 1-57167-141-2
Library of Congress Catalog Card Number: 96-67168

Book Layout: Michelle Summers
Cover Design: Deborah M. Bellaire
Developmental Editor: Maurey Williamson

Coaches Choice Books is an imprint of: Sagamore Publishing, Inc.
P.O. Box 647
Champaign, IL 61824-0647
(800) 327-5557
(217) 359-5940
Fax: (217) 359-5975
Web Site: http//www.sagamorepub.com

DEDICATION

This book is dedicated to all present and former University of New Mexico softball players who by their play, their dedication and their character have helped make our program a source of pride both for UNM and the state of New Mexico.

ACKNOWLEDGMENTS

We would like to give a special thanks to all those administrators and fans who stood by us and our program over the years, whose support and belief helped us to build a program we could all be proud of. In particular we would like to thank Linda Estes for her friendship and her support.

CONTENTS

PREFACE

Softball's Power Offense is a training manual designed to bridge the gap between teaching fundamentals and maximizing performance. This book will cover the complete scope of implementing an offensive strategy, from hitting to attacking a defense with aggressive baserunning.

The heart and soul of this book, as is true of any offense, is hitting. It was written to provide coaches at all levels with insights into analyzing hitters and methods to train and develop good hitters, both physically and mentally. These factors are accomplished through description, illustration and a better understanding of the skill of hitting. All instructions are for a right-handed hitter.

This book is for students of the game who want to think and want to learn. It describes our philosophy at the University of New Mexico, but every coach should develop their own approach and this book provides the knowledge to accomplish such a task.

CHAPTER 1

The Art and Science of Hitting

Hitting is the most difficult skill to master in the world of athletics. A hitter must master the physical fundamentals of the swing; develop the mental and emotional tools that will provide vital discipline and concentration; overcome any fear factor that may exist; and make smart choices on pitches, both in terms of location and movement.

The most important thing coaches can do is to educate themselves. There are many good books on the market, including books written by former players Charlie Lau (*The Art of Hitting .300*) and Ted Williams (*Science of Hitting*), and current Major Leaguer Wade Boggs (*Techniques of Modern Hitting*). Each one has its own philosophy and provides a different perspective. Young coaches need to study the ideas of professionals to gain a better understanding of the game. Interpretations often become exaggerations when coaches have only a superficial understanding of a philosophy.

The process begins with an understanding of the concepts, followed by an understanding of fundamentals and training. The art comes from the science, but it is useless if the athlete is not an educated hitter. Talent can win out, as demonstrated by professional baseball players who have natural ability that far outweighs their fundamentals. But for most people, success is based on developing solid fundamentals and being intelligent hitters.

The Performance Zone

Hitters need to realize that there is a "performance zone" that contains the perfect spot for hitting any pitch. No matter how hard hitters work on fundamentals, they still need to know the critical timing of the swing. More specifically, they need to know when to start the swing and where to make contact with the ball.

Wade Boggs briefly addresses this area in his book by calling it the "impact zone." Ted Williams concentrates more on the location of the pitch and approaches hitting by looking at the pitches he personally hit best. In other words, he focuses on pitch selection.

This chapter will expand on the "performance zone." Understanding this concept is important in the development of a great hitter. The basic premise is that the hitter must cover the plate. The hitting zone for each hitter is determined by bat length, arm length, position in the batter's box and the batter's strike zone.

The Hitting Diagonal: Fact and Fiction

On every swing the batter wants full arm extension on contact with the ball, without dropping the hands in a golf swing. That means on an inside pitch, the ball must be struck far out in front of the plate, while an outside pitch should be hit over the plate. In determining the proper contact point for balls that fall between these two extremes, coaches have drawn what they call a hitting diagonal. Depending on the individual coach's philosophy, the "line" that goes from the inside to the outside pitch is either a straight line or an angled line (refer to diagram 1-1).

Since the outside pitch should be hit over the plate, the line angles down sharply from the pitch that comes over the middle of the plate. Five softballs fit across the width of the plate, so when talking about pitch location, diagram 1-1 depicts where the ball travels across the plate. The hitter has to realize where to hit each pitch in relation to home plate, no matter if the coach believes the line is straight or angled.

The Inside Pitch
This is the pitch hitters must recognize quickly, because it is the pitch they must make contact with the farthest from the plate. The pitch that hits the inside part of the plate must be struck about three feet in front of the hitter's front foot in order for the hitter to have complete arm extension. When the ball is not hit in that area, hitters must bend their arms, or back off the plate in some manner in order to make contact at the end of the bat.

Middle of the Plate
This is the easiest pitch to hit. Hitters need to have their hands about a foot and a half in front of their front foot to have complete arm extension.

The Outside Pitch
Next to the middle of the plate pitch, this is the easiest pitch to hit. However, since hitters don't know how to hit this pitch, or because they lack patience, hitters tend to hit this pitch poorly. In this area, hitters must wait longer and hit the ball off the back leg while maintaining arm extension.

Where each hitter actually needs to make contact in relation to the plate depends upon where that hitter stands in the batter's box. Looking at the performance zone in more depth, the diagonal really becomes a plane, since the height of the ball, as well as its location, will affect where it needs to be struck. The plane is also determined by each hitter's strike zone. This diagonal plane actually creates a hitting zone where a wide variety of pitches pass through to be hit in a "perfect" spot for maximum performance.

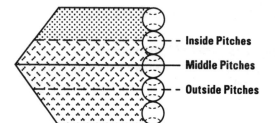

- Inside Pitches
- Middle Pitches
- Outside Pitches

Illustrating the Performance Zones Diagram 1-1

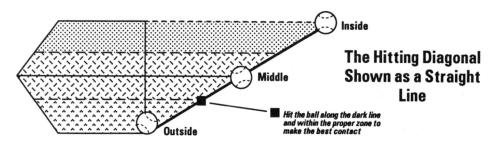

Inside

Middle

Outside

The Hitting Diagonal Shown as a Straight Line

■ *Hit the ball along the dark line and within the proper zone to make the best contact*

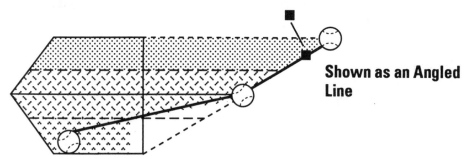

Shown as an Angled Line

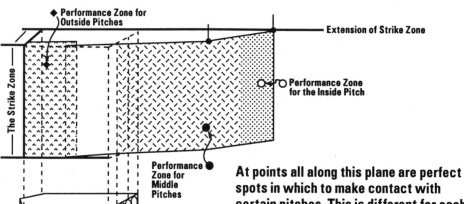

◆ Performance Zone for Outside Pitches

Extension of Strike Zone

The Strike Zone

Performance Zone for the Inside Pitch

Performance Zone for Middle Pitches

The Hitting Diagonal Combined with the Strike Zone

At points all along this plane are perfect spots in which to make contact with certain pitches. This is different for each hitter. The reason why this is so important is because this is the goal of hitting—to make perfect contact. Hitters need to visualize that all the physical, mental and emotional skills that come into play are designed for one purpose and that is to recognize the proper point of contact and figure out how to get the bat there at the same time the ball arrives.

Getting Physical
Diagram 1-2

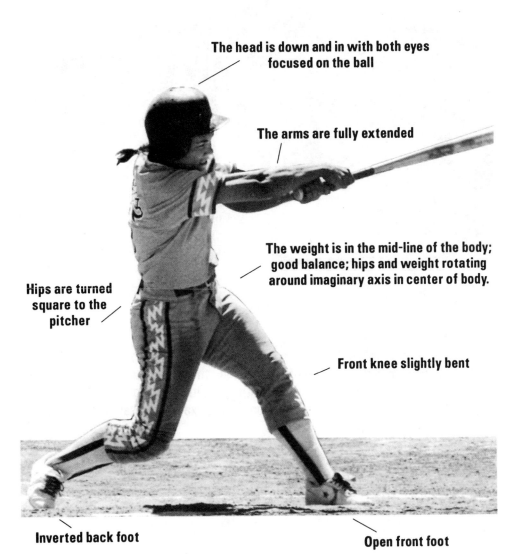

The head is down and in with both eyes focused on the ball

The arms are fully extended

The weight is in the mid-line of the body; good balance; hips and weight rotating around imaginary axis in center of body.

Hips are turned square to the pitcher

Front knee slightly bent

Inverted back foot

Open front foot

Hitting the Outside Pitch

Every cut should be taken the same, regardless of the location of the pitch. The subtle changes are in the position of the head and the arms. In this photo, the hitter is driving the outside pitch to right field. Both eyes are watching the ball. The hands have gone directly to the ball. The other basics are exactly the same as the ones from the photo in Diagram 1-2.

CHAPTER 2

Hitting Fundamentals From Bottom to Top

The Feet
The back foot should be square to the plate, or closed. The front foot should be open at a 45-degree angle or more to allow for a quick transition of the body through the swinging motion. This allows the hips and the lower body to move along with the upper body.

Taking a stride, hitters start with their feet a little more than shoulder width apart. The stride is about 6-12 inches past shoulder width, and does not include a weight shift to the front leg. The weight stays in the mid-line of the body.

The step with the front foot should be directly toward the pitcher every time. The key is plate coverage. Adjusting the step to the location of the pitch is not recommended because it is one more movement that can go wrong and hamper the swing. There is strength in repetitions, so the step should be kept the same.

The Legs
There should be a slight bend in the knees for a relaxed posture.

The Hips
For a smooth flow in the swing, it is necessary for the hips to follow the bat around the body. Usually this is a natural motion, hindered only by poor positioning of the feet.

The Front Shoulder
The front shoulder starts slightly down to counter dropping the hands when the swing starts. The shoulder opens naturally with the follow-through, not with the

initial action of the hand. When the shoulder is pulled out early, it pulls the hitter off the plate and often results in the hitter pulling the head and not seeing the ball all the way to the plate. The hitter always takes a direct line to the ball, bringing maximum force in one direction. When pulling away, a certain amount of that force is lost moving away from the ball.

The Hands
The grip recommended is the finger grip. Even if a traditional grip is used, the critical factor lies in proper knuckle alignment and bringing the hands to the ball. (Knuckle alignment will be discussed later.) A short compact cut with maximum hand speed is essential for a softball hitter. The bat head will follow the hands. Young hitters have trouble understanding hand speed, so coaches need to encourage them to swing harder.

Inward rotation (called the "launching position" by Charlie Lau) is also a technique that is often neglected. When a stride is taken, the hands are pushed back in a cocking action. If a hitter strides out, the hands start back. The left arm is not fully extended, but just pushed back far enough to create some tension in the front shoulder. The cocking action is back toward the catcher, not around the head.

When striding out, the hitter's hands will start back.

The Head
The head should be relaxed, with the chin slightly down. The head should be turned enough toward the pitcher to allow both eyes to have a clear view of the ball.

The Trunk
There should be a slight bend toward the plate, starting at the waist. A hitter should not start upright with the head and shoulders off the plate. Again, hitters should stay away from extremes.

The Stance
Comfort is the most important factor concerning the stance. Extremes are not good in any area. Some hitters may start from an extreme (bending way over), but come up to a hitting stance as the pitcher prepares to throw the ball. Hitters can start anywhere they want. It's where they end up when they initiate the swing that matters.

Weight Shift

The weight starts in the mid-line of the body or the back. During the swing the weight moves around and imaginary vertical axis through the center of the body. A typical problem is created when a hitter brings the weight forward to the front foot as the stride is taken. This causes the hands to move forward before the start of the swing, slowing down the hand speed by decreasing leverage.

The Hitting Sequence

The stance.

The swing.

The follow-through.

CHAPTER 3

Common Errors:
For Every Action, There's A Reaction

The key to coaching is not just seeing what went wrong, but being able to determine what led to the mistake. There are many reasons why a hitter may hit a pop-up, like slow hands, throwing the weight forward too soon, or hitting the ball over the plate.

When looking at a hitter, the coach must be able to see the whole picture, and determine what is leading to the problem. This is where photographs and videotapes are essential, since most young coaches don't have the experience or "trained eye" to detect problems. For every action, there's an equal and opposite reaction.

Common Problems with the Feet

What to look for: When the hitter is in the initial stance, the coach should look to see where the feet are pointing.

Reasons and causes: The feet are usually out of alignment because of a lack of attention. This may also occur with less confident hitters, since they tend to hit with only their upper body. Also, if young hitters have a compact stride that does not give them a strong balance point, they swing with little weight shift. Basically, the feet being out of alignment causes the hips to lock, preventing them from opening toward the pitcher. This also creates pressure on the front knee joint.

Making changes: One of the checkpoints in the stance should be feet alignment. The back foot is the most neglected checkpoint. The stride should be eliminated in the beginning working drills, while the feet are set properly. Initially, coaches concentrate too much on the hands when the lower body is the foundation of the swing. Coaches should look for that compact stride and recognize the timid hitter who tends to hit with only the upper body.

Front foot locked.

Back foot pointing toward catcher instead of perpendicular to plate.

Stepping in the Bucket
What to look for: Hitters moving the left part of their body away from the plate.

Reason and causes: This is caused by a fear element, or when the hitter is trying to create more bat speed by twisting the upper body. This results in a sweep swing.

Making changes: This is not so much a physical problem as it is a mental problem. Proper fundamentals should be developed through drills. Repetitions will help build confidence.

A hitter stepping in the bucket.

Overstriding
What to look for: The hitter is striding past the balance (stable) point.

Reasons and causes: This is caused by the hitter transferring weight to the front foot and the speed of the stride. The stride should be a controlled step, not a rushed lunge. This mistake ruins the rhythm of the swing and hurts the hitter in many ways.

Making changes: In a drill situation, the hitter should stride out. Next, the coach can

A hitter with the front shoulder up and the hands low.

progress to a drill where the hitter strides, stops (to check weight and step), and swings after a slight hesitation. Finally, the coach can allow the hitter to stride by working off of a batting tee.

Front Shoulder Up

What to look for: The front shoulder needs to be slightly lower than the back shoulder.

Reasons and causes: This is often caused by using a heavy bat. The higher the front shoulder is, the more likely the hitter will develop a hitch in the swing. A high front shoulder also forces the hands lower.

Making changes: Shoulder position should be part of a checklist when hitters get into their stance. The coach should work on pushing the hitter's hands up. (If the front shoulder is up, and a coach pushes the hitter's hands up, it will also bring up the arms to show the error.)

The Sweep Swing

What to look for: From the start of the swing the hands move toward the opposite batter's box, instead of toward the pitcher.

Reasons and causes: This may be caused by the hitter using a heavy bat or trying to create more bat speed. Hitters may be able to generate the same speed by sweeping, but the longer stroke takes more time. To hit a certain pitch, a sweep swinger will have to start the swing sooner (making quick decisions), meaning they are more susceptible to being fooled by change-ups or any movement pitches.

The swing sweep.

Making changes: Using a batting tee will help with concentration on the fundamentals of bringing the hands to the ball. The coach can also place a home plate by a fence, so when hitters swing, the bat will come into contact with the fence if they sweep.

Pulling Left Shoulder Out

What to look for: When the shoulder initiates bat movement, not the hands.

Reasons and causes: The hitter is trying to create more bat speed by using larger muscle groups. This causes the hitter to pull away from the plate, preventing good eye contact and lessening the force by which the ball is hit.

Making changes: This problem can usually be changed easily by having the hitter work off of stationary batting tools that emphasize fundamentals.

A hitter pulling the left shoulder out.

Improper Hand Position

What to look for: The hands in the stance should be held just above or just below the shoulder. Anything lower than that is not effective. The coach should also check to see if the hands are off the back shoulder or inside the back shoulder toward the mid-line of the chest. If the hands start forward, they can be corrected with inward rotation, but they should never stay forward. How far the hands should be away from the body varies for every hitter, but they should never be in an extreme position.

A hitter displaying improper hand position.

Reasons and causes: This can be caused when a young hitter uses a heavy bat because that forces the hands to be low and close to the body in order to handle the weight of the bat. Lack of inward rotation and having the front shoulder up will also cause improper hand positioning. When the hands start in the wrong position, they will obviously affect hand speed and the ability to bring the hands directly to the ball. Depending on the extremes, improper hand position could also lead to other problems, like hitching.

Making changes: Many times this problem is more mental than physical. The coach should go back to the hitter's basic alignment and focus on proper hand position in a variety of stationary drills. Many repetitions should be worked with the hands up and in a good position relative to the body.

Improper Bat Position
What to look for: The bat should be off the shoulder, but not wrapped around the head.

Reasons and causes: A hitter may try to create more torque or bat speed by winding-up. Improper bat position may also come from a misunderstanding of inward rotation, like cocking with the shoulders instead of the hands. A lot of hitters start with the bat in a variety of positions, but the coach should check to see where the bat is just before the swing. Poor bat position will increase the time it takes to bring the bat to the hitting area.

Improper bat position includes wrapping the bat around the head.

Making changes: Awareness again plays a major role. The hitter needs to work on drills where the concentration starts with a noting of proper bat position.

Improper Weight Shift
What to look for: A coach does not want a hitter moving the weight forward to the front foot. It depends on the individual hitter whether to start with the weight on the back foot or on the mid-line of the body.

Reasons and causes: This problem is tied closely to overstriding. Hitters try to increase bat speed, or stride out too aggressively and lose control, creating a variety of problems for hitters.

Making changes: The hitter should be started from a position with no stride, and hit off some stationary batting tools. Coaches can try the start-stop drill, where the hitter starts the swing, then stops and hesitates for a moment before finishing the swing. This makes hitters more aware of weight shift and the timing of the shift.

A hitter improperly shifting her weight forward.

Incorrect—the back foot is out with the hips locked.

Correct—the back foot is tilted and the hips follow through properly.

Incorrect—arms bent on an inside pitch.

Correct—arms extended on an inside pitch.

The Grip: Traditional and Finger Grips

What to look for: The three things to look for in the grip are knuckle alignment, holding the bat in the heel of the hand instead of the palm, and holding the bat too tightly or loosely.

Traditional grip.

Reasons and causes: The hitter will rotate the top hand so that the middle knuckle of the top hand is aligned with the bottom knuckle of the bottom hand. In a correct alignment, the middle knuckles of both hands should be aligned. The main problem with improper alignment is that it prevents a wrist snap. It may also cause the bat to "hop" over the ball since the wrist comes underneath the bat and, on contact in an attempt to snap the wrist, actually drives the bat over the ball. A tight grip tenses the muscles and slows the bat, while a loose grip weakens bat control. When the bat is held in the heel of the hand by the thumb, bat control is also decreased.

Making changes: The biggest factor in change is awareness.

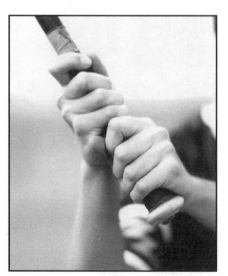

Finger grip.

The Finger Grip
The finger grip is recommended because of better bat control. It is better to hold the bat in the fingers because they have more dexterity. The finger (or golf) grip also covers a bigger surface of the bat, while keeping the fingers down at the bottom of the bat. This gives the hitter the advantages of choking up on the bat while still maintaining the length of the bat.

Progression to the Finger Grip

The following pictures depict the progression to the finger grip for a right-handed hitter. 1—The hitter should lay the bat across the fingers of the left hand, while angling the handle from the base of the little finger to the tip of the first finger. 2—The left hand should then be wrapped around the handle. 3—The hitter maintains the angle and creates a "V" by pointing the thumb and the first finger toward the right shoulder. 4—Maintaining these same angles, the hitter should then wrap the fingers of the right hand around the bat handle, but the little fingers should not be interlocked. 5—The hitter should keep a light grip. The left hand simply holds the bat, while the right hand initiates and directs the bat power.

1

2

3

4

5

CHAPTER 4

Making Changes: Training the Hitter

An understanding of fundamentals and common hitting mistakes is necessary for a coach to develop an eye for seeing mistakes and help the hitter work on a sound swing. It is important, however, that coaches to not attempt to train the "perfect hitter." Hitting is a matter of comfort, and all hitters have their own idiosyncrasies. Coaches should focus on major points that are affecting a hitter's performance in a negative way. Bad habits will be more ingrained with an older athlete, whereas coaches have a better chance of developing sound fundamentals with younger athletes.

Coaches should try not to change what is already working for hitters. The only time a coach changes a successful hitter is when that success is based more on facing inferior pitchers than on good fundamentals. Adjustments in cases like this are made for the future when the competition is much tougher.

As important as it is for coaches to develop an eye for technique, even the best coaches don't rely entirely on their own sight. Coaches can often utilize videotape and still photos. The less experience coaches have, the more they need to use visual aids to benefit both them and the athletes.

The basic philosophy in practice organization is to break down the hitter's swing as much as possible, and set up stations that will work on specific areas with as many repetitions as possible. Early training should be mainly drills, and gradually working up to hitting off pitchers. Drills should never be overlooked as even the best hitters need to polish up on their swing from time to time. During every drill coaches should maintain an attitude of quality over quantity, with hitters always swinging at full-speed. Instead of having hitters going through the motions, coaches can make each swing a learning experience. Athletes should know the purpose of each drill and know what they are trying to accomplish.

A coach should always use good judgment on when to criticize and when to encourage the hitter. Batting is a difficult skill, and staying positive with athletes and keeping them positive is a major goal. When hitters make consistent mistakes, coaches should explain again what is happening, along with complementing those things they are doing well as they grow as hitters. When hitters grow frustrated and discouraged they will quickly lose their aggression and confidence.

Coaches also need to know when to stay quiet. When hitters are batting off a pitcher during practice, they should be taught the same rules they need to use in a game, which are to clear their mind and look for the ball. It should not be a time to talk about fundamentals. Instruction should be kept to a minimum, with hitters being allowed to work on other aspects of hitting, like aggression and concentration. Whether it is during a game or a practice, the last place in the world for a lot of talk and instruction is in the batter's box.

Whenever a coach notices that a good hitter has become tentative (the hitter starts watching too many good pitches, or is always getting behind in the count), it is a good indication that the hitter needs a boost. A hit-and-run signal from the coach will free a hitter from any decision except to watch the ball. This practice has helped more than one hitter break out of a batting slump.

Batting Tools

Many batting tools can be used to train the hitter. There are many more on the market, and every coach needs to research available tools and decide what is best. Batting tools do not have to be expensive, they just need to be an effective way to teach a given fundamental. It is important to remember that instruction always comes first, and every swing should be taken with a purpose.

Soft Toss

One of the least expensive and best methods of teaching is the soft toss. The only equipment needed is a bat and a ball. The hitter can hit into a fence or out into the field. The purpose of the drill is to allow a hitter to isolate on fundamentals by hitting a slow moving ball. The tosser needs to be off to one side of the hitter at a 45-degree angle. The tosser should sit about seven feet from the hitter and toss the ball in front of the hitter. (The ball is tossed to the hitter, not at the hitter.) Common mistakes include having the tosser at a 90-degree angle (making the hitter hit the ball over the plate), and having the hitter take one swing after another as fast as possible (defeating the purpose of working on fundamentals).

Side view of the soft toss.

Back view of the soft toss.

There are many areas where hitters can focus their attention or work on their hand speed. The coach can toss the ball in one location to work on a single pitch, or mix it up and make the hitter react to a variety of pitches. The coach can also mark the ball with colors to help the hitter's concentration.

The Batting Tee

The batting tee is another inexpensive tool that is invaluable in the teaching process. Since some batting tees have the stems located on home plate, the coach should always use a second home plate as the guide for the hitter. Otherwise, the hitter will be taught to hit the ball over the plate. The batting tee pictured is the kind recommended because the stems are located in front of a plate and because it has multiple stems to provide a wide variety of pitches and drills.

Batting tee.

One way to use the batting tee is to place one ball simulating an inside pitch and placing another ball simulating an outside pitch. Using the principle of hands to the ball, the hitter is asked to hit the inside pitch first and then the outside pitch. A sweep swinger will always make contact with the outside pitch first because the bat is extended early. Another drill will have two stems placed in the middle of the plate with one hole separating them. Hitters are asked to hit the ball closest to them and drive it through the second ball. The key is to hit the middle of the ball.

The Juggs curve master batting machine.

Batting Machines

When training hitters, one of the most important tools is some type of batting machine. There are many on the market, like the Juggs Curvemaster and Juggs Junior for outside training, and a Granada Baseball machine for indoor training. The Granada machine is great for very young hitters. The Batting Tutor is very similar to the Granada, but is more portable and can throw a variety of pitches.

There are an endless number of fundamentals that can be developed with a batting machine. The Granada and Batting Tutor work with plastic balls from a shorter distance and help greatly with hand speed. Both machines guarantee a lot of swings for the hitter even in bad weather. When there is not a lot of wind, the battery-powered Batting Tutor is excellent for use outdoors and can travel easily to away games for batting practice.

The Batting Tutor batting machine.

The Juggs machines simulate hitting off a pitcher better than the other machines. A coach can adjust the speed, set the machines at 43 feet (or closer to work on bat speed), and set the machine to throw a variety of pitches. The important thing to remember is that the coach should never send a group of hitters to work off of a machine without first instructing them on exactly what they should be trying to accomplish. One drill may emphasize away pitches, while another may focus on inside pitches or curveballs. Every swing should be taken at full-speed and every drill should have a purpose.

Stationary Batting Tools

There are many tools now on the market that allow the hitter to work on fundamentals off of a stationary object. The string hitter permits hitters to hit a ball off the string just like a batting tee, or they can hit a moving object when a coach slides the ball at them with a wand. The speed can be adjusted by the coach.

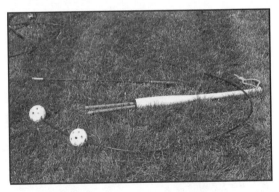

The string hitter.

The hitting stick is a safer version of hitting a ball on the end of a string. The coach swings the stick around for the hitter to hit.

The solo hitter suspends the ball so the hitter will receive a maximum number of swings.

The top hand bat is a bat with a weight in it that, on the swing, transfers from the middle of the bat to the end of the bat. The purpose is to teach top hand hitting and

The string hitter in use.

make the hitter swing hard in order to hear the weight "pop" as it hits the end of the bat.

All of these tools are excellent as long as the hitter uses them properly. They all work in a small area and lend themselves to circuit training, where the hitter moves from one drill to another while working on a variety of specific fundamentals. A coach who can isolate a certain problem and attack it with one drill is more likely to beat that problem than the coach who attempts to resolve the problem while dealing with the entire swing. The swing should be broken down before the tools to best address the problem areas are chosen.

The hitting stick.

It is important for a coach to understand time limits. There is a huge difference between a coach who has two hours once a week and only four weeks of practice before the first game, and a coach who has three hours five days a week and six months before the first game. Less time to prepare means there is less a coach can accomplish, and the more important it is for that coach to be organized. A priority list should be set for each skill. With a short period of time to practice, a hitter will not be able to make multiple changes. The younger hitter will generally be able to deal with less information, so the coach should keep it simple and always keep in mind what the age and talent of the athletes are.

A coach has to be the most adaptable person on the team, because every athlete and every situation requires a different approach. While fundamentals and a philosophy may stay the same, the approach and drills must always adjust to the situation.

Before and After—Three Players During Their Freshman Years and During Their Senior Years

The three following athletes all came into college as freshmen with many fundamental problems in their swing. All three started college as strong "potential" hitters, but would not have progressed if they were not able to master basic hitting fundamentals. That came with knowledge and many repetitions in practice. It is important for young athletes to understand they don't have to accept weaknesses, but rather they should correct those flaws and reach their potential.

Senior year

Freshman year

Senior Year

Freshman year

Senior Year

Freshman year

Hitting Drills

Drill #1: Stick Drill

Objective: To teach players how to hit on the end of the bat and increase their concentration.

Equipment: Any slender stick (doll rod, cut-off broom stick, etc.) with five inches of pipe insulation wrapped around the end; golfball-sized whiffle balls.

Description: A coach stands in front of the hitter and tosses the whiffle balls for that person to hit. The balls should be thrown down the middle of the plate so the hitter can focus on making contact at the end of the bat.

Coaching points:

• This serves as a great drill to improve hitters' concentration, along with showing them where on the bat they should hit the ball.

• Depending on the skill level of the individual hitter, the coach should also pay attention to other fundamentals, especially arm extension and normal bat speed.

Drill #2: Fence Toss

Objective: To work on a player's basic swing without other distractions.

Equipment: Reinforced fence; bucket of old softballs.

Description: The hitter should stand about 10 feet from the fence in a position to hit softballs into it. The coach stands in front and to the side of the hitter and tosses softballs in various locations in front of the hitter. The balls should be tossed with some loft so the hitter can explode into them and drive them into the fence with as many line drive shots as possible. The coach can isolate and work weak areas in the hitter's swing by controlling the location of each "pitch."

Coaching points:

• The coach should never rush the hitter. Time should be taken on each toss to utilize the best of the hitter's ability and the hitter's maximum hand speed.

• The coach should never stand directly opposite the hitter, but rather in front and off to the side of the hitter at about a 45-degree angle. This will help the hitter to better simulate the correct location at which to strike the ball.

Drill #3: Color Ball Drill

Objective: To increase the hitter's ability to focus on the ball.

Equipment: Any type of solid ball with a large colored dot on it, or a ball with colored seams.

Description: The coach can toss the ball from in front or from the side of the hitter, or use a batting machine to throw machine balls. The entire focus of this drill is to force hitters to recognize the color placed on each ball as they are preparing to hit it. They should call out the color when they see it and then make a decision on whether or not to hit the ball.

Coaching point:

- This drill is still effective with very young hitters during the fence toss drill. But older hitters need to be pitched to from a greater distance so they will be forced to pick up the color of the ball as it travels toward them.

Drill #4: Inside/Outside Drill

Objective: To show hitters the difference in timing between hitting an inside pitch and hitting an outside pitch.

Equipment: Several softballs; two pitching machines.

Description: This drill can be set up in a wide variety of ways. For young hitters, this drill works best with a coach tossing ten balls inside, and then tossing ten balls outside, while mixing in a lecture on how to hit each pitch and when to start the swing. For higher-skilled players, the drill works best if the coach sets up two machines on the field in front of the pitching rubber. One machine should be set up to throw inside pitches, while the other machine is set up to throw to the outside part of the plate. The coach should rotate a series of pitches from the machines to each hitter, while reminding the hitters where to hit the ball in each location. By seeing where the ball goes when they hit it, hitters receive immediate feedback on both correct and incorrect hits.

Coaching points:

• This is a great teaching drill for hitters who always try to pull the ball and for hitters who always try to hit to the opposite field.

• This can also be a very frustrating drill because athletes always try to work on their strengths. Pitchers will obviously try to always throw to a hitter's weaknesses. This drill illustrates why it is important for a hitter to be able to hit pitches in all directions.

Drill #5: Homerun Derby

Objective: To serve as a fun way for hitters to be encouraged to generate power and take big cuts.

Equipment: Bucket of balls and a protector fence for the coach who is tossing the balls.

Description: The team should be separated into two equal teams. Each hitter should receive five pitches from the coach, in any location they request. The idea is to see how many homeruns each individual and each team can generate.

Coaching points:

• The drill works best with a livelier ball or a small 11-inch ball.

• Younger players can create their own fence with cones.

Drill #6: Top-Hand Drill

Objective: To teach players to isolate their top hand in order to hit with it.

Equipment: Bucket of balls, a fence, and a bat with the handle cut off and taped.

Description: Similar to the normal fence drill, the coach tosses balls to a hitter, but the hitter may use only the right hand (for a right-handed batter) to strike the ball with the short bat. The coach should emphasize the hitter getting on top of the ball. This is a great drill for hitters who tend to pull through the hitting zone with their left side, or hitters who pull off the ball with the front side of the body. This drill teaches hitters to drive through the ball and stay on top of it.

Coaching points:

- The bat should not be too heavy for the hitter. It should be light enough for the hitter to swing it without a major effort.

- Hitters should not sweep at the ball, but instead go directly from their ear to the ball.

Drill #7: Batting Tee

Objective: To work on special areas of the swing.

Equipment: Batting tee, bucket of balls and a fence.

Description: A specific area of the hitter's swing should be emphasized, with the tee set for that location and height. For a set period of time the hitter should hit balls at that one location.

Coaching point:

• The batting tee is excellent for hitters of all ages. It provides an opportunity for hitters to take numerous swings, along with teaching both proper mechanics and where to hit certain pitches (location).

Drill #8: Playing the Count

Objective: To teach highly-skilled hitters how to hit off live pitching.

Equipment: Bucket of balls for the pitcher on the mound; big protector screen located behind the catcher.

Description: The on-deck batter and the coach should stand behind the screen while the pitcher throws game situations. The coach calls balls and strikes and talks to the hitter about decisions concerning what pitches to hit and when to start the swing. The hitter gets one at-bat and rotates behind the screen to watch the next hitter.

Coaching point:

- Perfecting the swing is only part of the battle with this drill. The hitter has to learn what the strike zone is, what pitches to hit, what pitches not to hit, and how to take advantage of the count. The mental side of hitting demands just as much work as learning the basic fundamentals of the swing.

Drill #9: Situation Drill

Objective: To simulate several game situations while the hitter is at the plate, like hitting, bunting, faking a bunt, the squeeze play and the hit-and-run.

Equipment: Bucket of balls, possibly a pitching machine on the pitcher's mound.

Description: Before each pitch, the coach calls out a task, like the hit-and-run. The pitch is made and the hitter has to respond with the appropriate action. For instance, on a hit-and-run the hitter must swing at even a bad pitch to protect the runner. On a sacrifice bunt, the hitter has to look for strikes, and attempt to not bunt a bad pitch. Each hitter should be given 10 game situations and then rotate on defense or on baserunning.

Coaching points:

- This drill works best if the coach controls it by throwing the ball, either overhand or underhand.

- The coach should be demanding and apply pressure on the hitter since the hitter faces pressure in every at-bat.

Drill #10: Fast Hands

Objective: To teach hand speed.

Equipment: The best tool is a Granada indoor hitting machine; bucket of whiffle balls.

Description: The hitter is asked to hit whiffle balls off of the machine. However, the machine should be set only a short distance away so the balls get on top of the hitter quickly. Whiffle balls help reduce the fear element.

Coaching points:

- The skill level of the hitter will dictate what kind of Granada hitting machine to use (baseball or softball) and the distance from the batter to the machine. The college athlete may stand 19-20 feet from the machine and hit the smaller baseball-sized balls, while the younger players may use the larger softball-sized balls and hit from a farther distance.

- The hitter should be able to hit the ball by generating hand speed. Hitters who are constantly bailing out or pulling off the ball, or trying to gain speed by throwing the body around, are either not ready for the hitting machine or need to be filmed to show them their improper adjustments. This is an effective drill, but if the coach does not use good judgment on each hitter, bad habits will be developed by the hitter and no hand speed will be built.

Hitting Questions and Answers

1. Should the hitter always stand at the front of the batter's box in order to hit pitches before they break?

Standing at the back of the box against a fast pitcher gives a hitter more time, but it also increases the likelihood of hitting a foul ball. Standing at the front of the batter's box gives hitters less time, but does give them the opportunity to hit the pitch before it breaks. Standing in the middle of the batter's box is preferred.

2. What is the advantage of an inside-out swing?

It is more of a controlled swing. All swings really start inside-out, but the hands should then explode to the ball.

3. Should a hitter use a heavy bat to generate more power?

No. Bat speed and the point where the bat contacts the ball is more important.

4. Instead of trying to hit the ball hard, isn't it better to try making contact by slowing down the hands?

No. A hitter who tries to do that will usually hit the ball over the plate. It is difficult to judge the speed of the ball and slowly move the bat to make contact.

5. What is the difference between bottom and top hand hitting?

Technically, the swing should be a collaboration between both hands. The top hand will dominate and help result in better bat control.

6. Do hitters lose the ability to hit with power if they use the finger grip?

No, because they maintain bat speed and leverage while increasing bat control. The better consistent hitters are at hitting the middle of the ball, the more power they will generate.

7. Is it okay for a hitter to separate the hands on the bat?

Yes. It is similar to choking up on the bat.

8. How close should a hitter stand to the plate?

This can't be generalized because it varies from hitter to hitter. The main point should be plate coverage.

9. Is it bad to start with the bat laying on the hitter's shoulder?

It isn't important where the bat starts. What matters is where it ends up just before hitting the ball. Like striding out, the advantage is that it solves one problem (hitching), so the hitter does not have to think through that process at the plate.

10. What is the difference between a level swing and a chop?

By swinging down with a slight chop, the hitter hits the top and middle of the ball more often, resulting in more line drives and ground balls. With the level swing (especially against pitches like the rise ball), the hitter will hit the bottom half or middle of the ball more often. Most outs come on fly balls, whereas most hits come on line drives and ground balls.

CHAPTER 5

The Young Hitter

Working with very young hitters is rewarding, but it presents unique problems for coaches. The first thing coaches should know is to never sell young hitters short and assume they can't handle the fundamentals. They should be taught the same basics that older hitters learn, but coaches should lower their expectations. Young hitters won't be as consistent and a coach can't make the same demands, but they can learn the same basics. The photos in this chapter are taken of a four-year-old and a six-year-old as they attempt certain skills.

At a young age in the early stages of development, athletes are usually not very strong. Young hitters often start out with a bat that is much too heavy for them to handle, leading to many hitting errors. A heavy bat will cause a hitter to sweep and use the body instead of the hands. It will also affect the speed of the swing and generally keep hitters from successfully hitting the ball. Hitters should always use a bat they can handle. There are plenty of plastic bats and smaller wooden and aluminum bats on the market that young hitters should be able to swing efficiently.

The second area of concern for young hitters is concentration. Anyone who has worked with young children knows that their attention span is not very long. Kids are long on action and short on listening. Instruction needs to be short and very specific. Young people also don't retain information well or transfer instruction from one drill to another. Instructions should be repeated often and, when moving from one drill to another, coaches should not expect hitters to carry the same principle with them from the previous drill.

Coaches can start with the basics, but should not take the fun out of hitting by giving the hitters too much information. The coach starts by setting the hitters' feet in proper position and having them stride out, rather than dealing with taking a stride. The hitters should then bend a little at the waist and knees while working on their hand position, making sure to keep the hands up high. The coach should show them the proper movement to the ball, and tell them to watch the ball while displaying little or no head movement. Coaches should explain to the hitters where the ball needs to be hit—the performance zone.

Training the Young Hitter

Coaches should start with the most simple basics and a stationary object, taking the time to set the hitters for each swing. Plastic bats and balls are highly recommended for the youngest hitters because they are easier to handle. The age will vary for each hitter, but once they are able to play catch (even if they don't always catch the ball), they can try hitting a moving ball. Coaches can start with a plastic ball and toss it at the bat from a very short distance. At first the coach can stand behind the hitters and help them swing, but the hitters should be on their own as soon as possible.

There are many games on the market for kids, so the coach can be creative in the drills that are provided. The batting tee and the string hitter are great progressive tools. The string hitter allows the hitter to start stationary and then progress to hitting a moving ball.

The stance.

The swing.

The stance.

The swing.

Drills for Young Hitters

Fist Drill
The players should stand in their normal batting stance without a bat. Their hands should be held where they normally are, and they should make a fist with the right hand. The coach stands in front of them, holding up a pillow or hand in front of each individual hitter to simulate a pitch coming from the pitcher. On command from the coach, hitters will throw their fist directly out to the ball (pillow) to hit it. This drill teaches top hand hitting and the principle of hand to the ball.

Shadow Drill
When practicing outdoors, hitters should stand with the sun directly behind them. The shadow of the head should be projected on the ground in front of the hitter. As the hitter takes a swing, the coach should note the difference between where the head starts and ends. This drill will show if the hitter is lunging.

Bat Behind Hips
A bat should be placed behind a hitter's hips or waist, and the hitter should secure it with the hands or wrist. The hitter then takes a normal hitting stance with the lower body. On command from the coach, the hitter swings the hips (and the bat) to simulate hitting the ball. The coach should check the position of the feet and legs, making sure the weight stays in the mid-line of the body.

Bat behind the hips—front view.   **Side view.**

Cut-Off Bat
A bat should be cut off just below the trademark. The hitter should assume normal position and hold the bat in only the right hand. The hitter works hitting the ball off a tee or in soft toss to teach top hand hitting and hand to the ball. The bat should not be too heavy.

Stride-Stop
The hitter should take a stride but no swing. After coming to a stop, the coach should go through a checklist of the head, hands, shoulders, hips and feet position. If everything is in alignment, the coach then gives the command to hit. This drill forces the hitter to recognize good and bad points at a critical time just before the swing. This is an effective drill for any hitter.

CHAPTER 6

The Mind Game

Once hitters know their goal (to hit the ball in the performance zone), and once they develop the fundamentals to accomplish their goal, they must master a third area, the area that controls the mind and the emotions. In many ways, success in hitting is based in great part on a hitter's ability to stay focused on the task at hand. Coaches talk all the time about focus and concentration, but what really matters is that a hitter must be able to block out all sights, sounds and thoughts, and tunnel in on the ball as it is delivered from the pitcher. The entire world must be compressed into a narrow vision of the ball as it reaches the critical point where it must be struck. Hitting is about developing good habits, and mental habits are just as much a part of the process as the physical habits are.

The Process

1. In the dug out—A good hitter studies the pitcher and the umpire, looking for tendencies and measuring up the competition. Hitters should learn as much as possible before their at-bat.

2. On deck—The process of tuning out begins. The hitter doesn't visit with other players, but instead works on relaxing and tuning in the main points of emphasis.

3. Signal—Once hitters receive the signal from the coach and step into the batter's box, they should click into the hitting zone.

Concentration is critical for a hitter.

From that point, the focus is on hitting the next pitch. Hitters should step into the box quietly and under control, while clearing their mind.

4. The batter's box—This is the hitter's sanctuary. Hitters are prepared to attack the next pitch and will not back off until they determine that it is not the pitch they want to hit. Hitters should be aware of the count, but the focus should be on one task—swinging the bat to meet the ball in a given point in the performance zone.

5. Ball is released—The mind takes over the body. The stride is taken, the hands are cocked and the fingers are relaxed around the bat. The mind makes the decision on the pitch, and either sends the message to attack or winds down and waits for the next pitch.

6. If the decision to swing is made—The commitment is complete. The mind focuses the body on drawing all the aggression to one point. If the body has been trained properly, all the energy and power will be directed along the hands

to the ball, with no parts of the body hindering the smooth flow of strength and speed.

7. Once contact has been made—The task is not finished until the follow-through drives the bat through the ball and around the body.

Knowing What Pitch to Hit

The perfect hitter with the perfect swing who has a good understanding of the performance zone should be able to hit every strike equally well. But that person does not exist. All hitters have certain pitches they hit better than others. Ted Williams drew a chart describing all the strikes and assigning batting averages to each spot, as if he hit that pitch every time. Knowing what pitch a hitter excels at, instead of just going to the plate as a free swinger, can make a big difference in the batting average. That is why it is so important for hitters to be ready to hit the first pitch and each one thereafter. Once hitters fail to swing at their best pitch, or miss it, they may never see that pitch again and the advantage goes to the pitcher. When hitters realize what pitches they hit best, they need to lay off other pitches until they see that one.

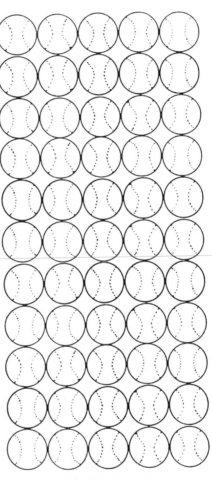

Sample softball hitting chart.

Playing the Count

When hitters are ahead in the count, they are in control and can afford to be more selective about pitches they choose to swing at. When hitters are behind, and obviously with two strikes, they have to widen the selection and just hit strikes. On a two balls and no strikes count, hitters should never pop up on a rise ball or ground out on a curveball that breaks away from them. This is where intelligent hitters use their fundamentals and their mind to be successful over talented players who make poor decisions. Some hitters get into bad habits of swinging at bad pitches in practice or against inconsistent pitchers. A coach needs to initiate that discipline right away. What is practiced will always show up in games.

Studying the Pitcher

Hitters need to scout pitchers. They should know what to expect and how to beat them. If hitters are facing a pitcher with one main pitch (rise, drop), then they already know how to approach that pitcher. For instance, with the rise ball pitcher, a hitter needs to lay off high pitches and make the pitcher throw the ball for strikes.

Other pitchers develop patterns, like throwing a good strike on the first pitch, or throwing pitches in a certain order, either by location or types of pitches. A pitcher may always throw a change-up at the beginning or at the end of a count. All of these facts can help the hitter.

How much control a pitcher has will also determine a strategy. If a pitcher has great control, a hitter needs to be more aggressive. If a pitcher has control problems, the hitter needs to be more selective, because that kind of pitcher will usually make a big mistake or may walk the hitter more often. Coaches need to teach hitters to be aware of pitchers so that the mind can help the body react to pitches.

Umpires

The strike zone is defined by the rule book, but what the umpire calls in the game is what matters. Hitters can never let an umpire take the bat out of their hands, and coaches should never let players concentrate on the umpire. Players should direct their attention to what it takes for them to be successful. When an umpire is inconsistent, hitters must widen their strike zone and hit strikes. Hitters can't afford to complain about what they can't control. They must focus on the ball and stay aggressive.

Emotion

A hitter must have controlled aggression. Emotion is very important, but it must always be kept under control. Emotion should always work for a hitter, and not detract from concentration or judgment.

Teaching Hitters How to Hit a Variety of Pitches

Players should cock the bat and wait until the last possible second to swing. This gives the batter more time to judge speed and movement. Hitting off a variety of pitchers in practice is very important because it helps hitters recognize spins. The more swings a hitter takes at the plate the better.

The Change-Up

Keeping the hands back gives the hitter more time to pick up the ball and its speed. It is the toughest pitch to hit. If hitters can keep their hands back, even if they are fooled on the pitch, they can at least explode with the bat and make contact.

Chopping the riseball.

The Curveball
Patience is the key. A hitter must recognize the movement and wait to hit the ball over the plate and off the back leg. A hitter can hit the ball before or after it breaks.

The Screwball
The key is again to recognize the ball movement and to have the hand speed to attack the ball. Hitters must realize that the ball is tailing inside and they must speed their hands up just as they would on any inside pitch.

The Drop
The mistake most hitters make with this pitch is that they drop their hands to the ball and then pull their body up and away from the ball. This causes the hitter to top the ball. The hitter needs to drive the bat through the center of the ball, staying with the pitch all the way.

Teaching Techniques

Duplicating a game situation is the best way to teach. Hitting off a variety of pitchers is very helpful. Having batting machines that can simulate pitches also works well.

There are many other techniques that will help batters, like visualization, having players hit balls with color marks on them, keeping a radio on or having the players talk around a hitter at the plate to help teach blocking out of noise, and practicing no-talking in batting practice for the hitter and the on-deck player. Other beneficial practices include always calling balls and strikes like in game situations, informing hitters when they let good pitches go by or when they swing at bad pitches, using baseballs and baseball bats to practice hitting a smaller object, and always keeping game situations between hitters and pitchers competitive, not recreational.

CHAPTER 7

Angle Bunting Off The Pivot

Every offense needs to have the capability of moving baserunners into scoring position or keeping defenses honest with the threat of a drag bunt. These are basic skills that every player needs to develop, whereas push bunting and the slap bunt are additional skills.

Just like hitting, the key to bunting is the player being in the proper position. Most unsuccessful bunts are the result of dropping the head of the bat and bunting the bottom half of the ball, or simply not being out soon enough to be in a position to control the pitch. That is why angle bunting off the pivot is taught. This technique minimizes movement by having the hitter rotate on the toes with no step. It also eliminates pop-ups by utilizing the 45-degree bat angle.

Body Position

The hitter stands in the front of the batter's box and pivots on the balls of the feet, shifting 75% of the weight to the front foot. The bat should be dropped to a 45-degree angle. The head of the bat should be brought forward just in front of the face, and the hitter should bend and relax at the knees.

Side view of the angle bunt.

Bat Position

The bat should cover the entire plate and should continue to be held at the 45-degree angle in front of the plate.

Hand Position

The hands should be held away from the body. The top hand is held a little more than halfway up the bat. Both hands can be moved up the bat, or they can be split. The elbows should be bent, with the bat held approximately one-half of an arm length away from the body. The bat should be held loosely with the top hand to avoid too much resistance when the ball hits the bat.

Head Position

The head is held almost directly behind the bat, and the hitter should watch the ball hit the bat.

Front view of the angle bunt.

Directing the Bunt

The bunt is directed with the bottom hand. If the ball is pushed with the right hand, the resistance that exists with a tight grip causes the ball to jump off the bat since the bunter is actually punching the ball, not bunting it.

To place the ball down the first base line, the bottom hand should be pushed out and away from the body, while always maintaining the 45-degree bat angle. To place the ball down the third base line, the bottom half of the bat should be pulled toward the body, while again keeping the 45-degree angle.

Bunters should have soft hands, but having them too soft is not good. Bunters should not slap at the ball or give too much and bring the hands into the body when the ball makes contact with the bat. They simply need to maintain the proper angle and let the ball drop off the bat. Using the bottom hand to direct the ball will help keep the top hand relaxed and allow for softer bunts.

Bunters should be in the front part of the batter's box to give them the maximum amount of fair territory to use. They should stand close to the plate, with the left foot almost touching home plate so they can cover the entire plate with the bat. This stance minimizes bat movement, gives bunters a clear view of the strike zone, and allows them to see the ball clearly as it comes to the plate. Traditionally the bunter's head is held above the bat, but in this style the head is held almost directly behind the bat to provide the best possible view of the ball.

When first teaching this method, coaches should have the bunters predetermine which direction they want to bunt the ball, and then have them push the bat in that direction. This helps bunters get over the fear element of having the ball come at them. Once they seem comfortable, they should soften the hands.

One of the most overlooked fundamentals of bunting is the body position. The hands should only move slightly, and the body should only raise or lower a short distance in any bunt. Coaches need to make sure the front foot is closer to home plate than the back foot is so that when bunters rotate (pivots) on their toes, the bat will cover home plate and bunters will stay balanced. The body should be in a position to sprint down to first base. If bunters over-rotate their knees, they will end up facing the pitcher and their bat will be covering their body instead of the plate. This forces bunters to reach for all strikes.

Front view of the outside pitch being bunted down the first base line.

Side view of the outside pitch being bunted down the first base line.

Front view of the inside pitch being bunted down the third base line.

Side view of the inside pitch being bunted down the third base line.

Common Errors

Coming Down Too Late

One of the most common errors is for bunters to come down from a hitting position to a bunting position too late. This rushes bunters and often times they end up sweeping or slapping at the ball, instead of coming to a stop and letting the ball fall off the bat. When proper timing is demonstrated, bunters come down as quickly as possible, with time left to set still for an instant before having to make contact with the ball.

Dropping the Hands

Many bunters drop their hands too low (down by their knees). This puts the bat in an awkward position and places the head too far above the bat, making it more difficult for the bunter to determine balls and strikes. In this position, bunters do not watch the ball come off the bat, and often times leads to them dropping the head of the bat.

The hitter dropping the hands.

Stiff Body

Bunters who seem to be afraid of the ball tend to keep their body stiff. This hurts their ability to efficiently move to the ball since they are trying to force the hands and the bat to do all the work. This problem causes bunters to be very awkward and slow.

Over-pivoting.

Over-Pivoting

When bunters pivot down from the batting position, they want to line up their body as if they are about to sprint down to first base. If they over-pivot, they will be facing the pitcher with the bat covering the body instead of the plate. This problem becomes worse if bunters start with their left foot back from home plate, because that prevents them from covering home plate.

Not Maintaining Bat Angle

One of the keys to the style of bunting described in this chapter is maintaining the bat angle through the execution of the bunt. Young hitters have a tendency to start with the 45-degree angle, but then drop the head of the bat as they bunt. This is especially true when they are thrown low pitches. Instead of dropping the body to cover low strikes, the bunter will drop the head of the bat and pop-up the ball.

Common Batting Errors

The batter dropping the head of the bat.

The angle of the bat is too great.

The bat is behind the head.

The bat being held flat.

The hitter standing too far away from the plate.

Teaching Bunting By Progression

The first step to successful bunting is to teach the fundamentals. Hitters should start with a bat in their hands, and then drop down on command to a bunting position. When they are able to do that, the coach should take away the bat and have the hitters catch a ball (or knock it down) with their right hand. The hand always moves with the fingers pointing up. Rotating the fingers down is the same as dropping the head of the bat. Coaches can move from that drill to drills where hitters bunt off a soft toss from the coach, where they bunt off a pitching machine, and finally where they bunt off a pitcher. How quickly players move through the progression depends upon their ability.

Low-pitch catching.

Low-pitch bunting.

Catching drill.

Bunting off a soft toss.

Drag Bunt From the Right

In the recent trend of the bunter/slapper, many coaches have forgotten about bunting from the right side. It is still a very effective weapon and should be taught to all hitters. An infield defense will key on a left-handed bunter, but players who hit from the right side can still produce the element of surprise, especially if they are good hitters.

There are many styles of bunting for a hit, but consistency in technique is important, so bunters should use the same basic style when they are sacrificing and when they are drag bunting. The major differences are in timing and footwork.

While the bunter who is sacrificing gets down early as the pitcher releases the ball, the drag bunter will wait until the pitch is closer to the plate. One of the typical errors is to bunt the ball over the plate. In drag bunting, the hands and the bat should still be in front of the body and home plate, not over the plate. That way, the ball can be bunted away from the body and allow for a quick release out of the box.

In order to position their body, bunters may either step across home plate with the back foot, making sure they don't touch the ground until after contact with the ball has been made, or they may execute a little hop-step. During the hop-step, bunters shift their weight to the back foot and then step forward (in a rocking motion) to the front foot as the bat is making contact with the ball. This is all accomplished in one simultaneous motion. Inside pitches are contacted in front of the body and are usually bunted down the third base line. Outside pitches are bunted off the front corner of the plate and are normally directed down the first base line.

Developing the timing for the drag bunt requires much practice. Since bunters are waiting longer before making contact with the ball, they should have a good view of balls and strikes, and they should only bunt good pitches. Bunters may predetermine where they want to bunt the ball, or they may bunt it where it is pitched.

Bunting Questions

1. If the hitter moves to the front of the batter's box, won't that tip the defense off that the hitter is going to bunt?

No. As long as the hitter steps completely out of the box, and then takes up the new position, most defenses won't even notice the change.

2. What are hitters doing wrong when they try to angle bunt, but keep popping-up the ball?

Most people who are learning to angle bunt start from the bunting position, but as they attempt the bunt, they drop the end of the bat. To prevent pop-ups, batters must maintain the 45-degree angle throughout the entire bunting process.

3. In sacrifice situations, batters may feel like they are swinging at the pitch instead of bunting it. How can they have softer hands?

In the sacrifice situation, the body and the bat should be still on impact. One of the typical mistakes for bunters is to come down to the bunting position too late. They then end up punching at the ball instead of waiting for it and giving with the impact when it hits the bat. Gripping the bat lightly in the fingers will also help create soft hands.

4. Why do seemingly good bunters consistently pop-up low pitches?

These bunters may be dropping the head of their bat, or the problem may be in their legs. On low strikes, bunters bend their legs and bring their whole body down to bunt. If they bunt with stiff and straight legs, the only way they can bunt a low strike is to drop the bat. The bunters should relax and move up and down the strike zone, making sure low pitches are strikes.

5. Why do some players run into the bunt when they are drag bunting?

Often times when drag bunting, the bunter forgets to get the hands out in front of the body, meaning the ball will be directed away from the path of the bunter. Bunters will often keep the hands and the bat close to the body, which handcuffs bunters/baserunners as they try to get out of the batter's box. Bunters can still have soft hands and place the ball where they want.

6. Why do a bunter's hands need to be placed close together on the bat?

If the hands are too far apart on the bat, bat control is greatly decreased.

7. How close to home plate should the bunter stand?

For the right-handed batter, the left foot should be right next to the plate and the right foot should be back off a couple of feet to provide stability. This position allows bunters to completely cover home plate when they are down in the bunting position.

8. What can a player who is afraid of bunting do to gain confidence?

This is a common problem. The basis of bunting comes from good fundamentals and understanding how to control the ball (and not letting the ball "attack" or get on top of the bunter). Bunters with fear issues need to bunt plastic balls while they are working on their skills in order to build confidence. When initially working on bunting, players should not concentrate on soft hands, but rather on taking a more aggressive attitude to push the bat at the ball until they feel confidence that they are in control.

9. Why do good hitters have to learn how to bunt?

There are times when it is in the team's best interest for a batter to move a runner over into scoring position. The best hitters are only successful three or four times out of 10 times at-bat, but there is no reason why a bunter can't be successful nine times out of 10-bunting situations. These are important percentages for a coach and the team.

10. In bunting situations, the corner players always charge and tend to get the lead out anyway, so why shouldn't the hitter just swing away?

It is the coach's job to take advantage of the defense. If a team always charges hard, then the coach may adjust in a number of ways, including hitting away or teaching bunters how to slap or fake bunt. Making adjustments is just a part of competing, but it doesn't diminish the importance of a player being able to sacrifice bunt when called upon by the coach.

CHAPTER 8

Teaching Sprinting

One of the most essential skills in softball is sprinting. Oddly enough, though, it is often one of the most neglected skills. Every aspect of the game requires good sprinting skills, from baserunning to defensive movement to the base or ball. Women, in general, have been taught very little about running techniques and seem to have a poor image of themselves in this aspect of the game. All athletes can improve their running skills and become better all-around players.

Like every other skill that is taught, there must be a commitment in both practice and in games. The first phase starts with knowledge and observance of good sprinting form. Since this is a specialized area, someone like a track coach can be brought in for the initial instruction and all demonstrations. This person can walk the players through the drills, and work with them individually to show them how they can improve their running form.

Proper running should be emphasized and practiced from that point. Information should be repeated and practiced until players know it as well as any other skill they are trying to master. Players should be timed when they first come into the program and at various times after that to see their improvement. Conditioning is not approached as a necessary pain, but rather as a means to excel.

The Basics of Running

Everyone is born with different running skills and natural speed. Softball players are not track athletes, and in many cases they are not built like sprinters. But that doesn't mean they can't be efficient runners. The first issue in softball is to get the players in good physical shape. For some reason, especially with younger coaches, conditioning is neglected and, as a result, their softball players are in poor physical shape. A good coach spends time talking to the players about their health, nutrition and conditioning, along with developing a program that will help each individual.

An infielder making a running catch on a pop-up.

Two views of the spring harness.

The second issue is to teach players about explosion and running hard. Most coaches never address the issue of teaching their players what "full speed" really means, and it's safe to say that most women do not run at full speed unless they are pushed to do so. Poor mechanics, lack of knowledge and lack of emotion lead to a mediocre effort that may not even be recognized by the athlete.

An excellent training tool to use is a speed harness, like the Gerber Super Sprint Trainer. Basically this tool simulates running up and down hills. A player straps on a harness with a thick 25-foot long rubber hose that is attached to a post. The hose provides resistance as the runner moves away from the post. At a point about 65 feet from the post, the runner turns around to face the post and runs full-speed toward it. The taut tubing will actually pull the runner along, increasing the runner's speed.

Players can also run through sand since that builds strength and forces the runner to work hard. Other methods a coach can devise may include having the players run races to create a more competitive situation where a coach wants a faster runner to "push" a slower runner. All of these methods are based on teaching runners they can run faster.

A player running in sand.

The Proper Techniques

Once runners know that they have some untapped speed in them, it is time to break the skills down and demonstrate the proper techniques.

1. Players should run without tightening and raising the shoulders, without clenching the fists, and without a stiff neck or their head back.

2. The hands and arms should move back and forth in a plane by the body, not across the body. A crossing movement with the arms throws the momentum and weight off-line. The hand comes in front of the body, then back toward the hip area, driving the elbow back. Some people run with very short, choppy arm movements that hurt drive and rhythm.

3. Bringing the heel to the butt is how track coaches describe the movement of bringing the foot off the ground. Runners should be light on their feet, running on their toes (never on the heels) and stepping as if they are running on hot coals. There should be a rapid movement of the feet picking up the heels and knees high off the ground.

4. The rhythm of all the body parts working together is a key to running. If the arms are slow and move across the body, it will affect the runner's speed. The arms should move in conjunction with the legs. As the right arm goes up, the left leg comes up, and vice versa.

Drills

1. Players sit on the ground with their legs out and hands and arms in a sprinting position. They should start moving the hands back and forth as rapidly as possible until the body actually starts bouncing off the ground.

2. In short lines, the players start marching slowly, working on coordinating the arms and legs, and having good body position. They should increase the speed of the march but should not lengthen the stride. As a variation, the coach can have players start slowly and then gradually build up to running in place at full-speed.

The sprint skip drill.

3. The players skip about 60 feet, but it should be a power skip where they try to gain as much height as possible.

4. Players stand in a line with their arms by their sides. On command from the coach, they start to fall forward, catching themselves just as they lose their balance. At that point they should go immediately into a sprint, trying to generate as much quickness as possible.

5. Players alternate between a slow jog and full speed in short intervals.

General Practice Methods

In the quest to teach better team speed and explosiveness, a system based on plyometrics can be used along with various drills to best teach the skills. The following are some of those drills.

Working out in sand.

1. Running through a sand pit, starting from a dead stop.

2. Running full-speed through a series of wooden blocks about eight inches high in order to make runners pick up their feet and knees.

3. Trying to gain as much height as possible over a 60-foot distance by power skipping.

4. Bounding from one area to another, trying to gain as much distance as possible.

5. Step-ups on a box that is about two feet high. Players should generally start with about 50 step-ups per leg.

Running hurdles.

Step-ups on a box.

6. Hopping up on a box that is about two feet off the ground, and then jumping down off the other side. Jumpers bend the knees upon landing and then try to jump as high as they can.

7. Jumping rope, either stationary or moving.

8. Jogging and sprinting using the sprint harness, usually in sets of five.

9. Players starting with both feet together, then jumping and bringing both knees up to their chest, or as high as they can.

10. Cone jumps can be set in a variety of ways. The runner has to jump over an obstacle and then begin quick starts.

11. Bouncing on a trampoline and using a variety of movements.

Jumping rope.

CHAPTER 9

Baserunning

Baserunning starts from the minute a hitter hits the ball. Running the bases is one of the most exciting and fun aspects of softball, yet many runners are underachievers. A good baserunner is a smart runner who challenges the defense and always tries to take the extra base. The runner should always run at full-speed and stay alert.

The Art of Taking the Extra Base

On all ground balls, the hitter turned baserunner should run down the baseline at full-speed and not slow down until running past first base. When beating out an infield hit, a runner should never lunge in the final step or slide into the base. The base should be hit like a sprinter hits the finish line tape.

After hitting a line drive or a fly ball, runners should always assume they will get a double, and make an arc to cut around first base at full-speed. If runners slow down or stop, they greatly decrease their chances of taking second base should a mistake be made by the defense. When there is doubt or a sudden stop is necessary, runners should always slide.

When hitters get a base hit and a runner is on second, they should assume they will continue to second base until they see that the throw will be cut-off.

When at first base in a sacrifice situation, runners should assume they will slide at second base. They should look to see if the ball is bunted down, and when approaching second base, look to see if someone is covering third base. If the play is not at second, smart runners may be able to take an extra base by continuing to third.

When at second base, runners should look to see who is covering third base. If the shortstop is standing too close to second, or if the third baseman is not alert, there may be an easy opportunity to steal. Even if the shortstop and the third baseman seem alert, the pitcher and the catcher may not be paying enough attention.

When scoring from second base, the runner should cut third base at full-speed until told by a coach to stop. The coach should be positioned down the third base line. Coaches make decisions based on what the defense is doing, and should assume all runners are maintaining their speed.

Checking the defense.

Runners have to notice where the fielders are positioned, so that when a hit occurs, a quick decision can be made on whether or not it will be a hit. Runners should try to pick up the ball as soon as they can and make quick decisions. Indecision usually results in an out. Runners should never hesitate.

When at third base, runners should assume there will be a passed ball or some other infield error. They should never be caught by surprise. On short fly balls, runners can fake an attempt to score in order to draw a throw and maybe force a defensive error.

Runners on base should always be aware if the pitchers and catchers, or other infielders, are paying attention. There may be an opportunity to steal a base.

With two out, baserunners take off on contact. No matter whether the hit appears to be an easy out or not, they should run at full-speed and continue to run hard until told to stop by the coach. An out should never be assumed, but an error should be.

General Rules

1. When there are runners at second base and third base with less than two outs, the runner at third should try to score on an infield hit.

2. When on base and less than two outs, runners need to make sure the ball is down or through the infield before leaving for another base. Runners need to be aggressive, but not reckless.

3. When at first base and a ground ball is hit to the second baseman, the runner should not run into a tag and give the defense an easy double-play.

4. When at first base and a left-handed batter is at the plate, the runner should shorten the lead to prevent a line drive double play, in case the ball is hit hard to the right side.

5. With two outs and a full-count on the batter, the runner takes off with the pitch.

6. Leads should be taken in the baseline. After all, the shortest distance between two points is a straight line.

What Smart Baserunners Should Know

—the number of outs
—the inning
—the score
—the defensive alignment
—the strength of the outfielders' arms
—the strength of the catcher's arm
—whether or not the opposing team has a pick-off play
—where the ball is at all times
—the speed of the baserunners ahead of them
—who on the opposing team accepts the throw in stealing situations

Baserunning Drills

Drill #1: Circuits

Objective: To learn the fundamentals of running the bases, as well as conditioning.

Description: The team starts at first base. The first runner sprints down to first base, with each successive runner following. A short space should be left between each runner. Runners jog back to home plate and then repeat the sprint, only this time they should run a double. The group should then jog back to home plate and run out a triple and finally a home run.

Coaching point:

- This is a great conditioning drill, but baserunning fundamentals should not be forgotten.

Drill #2: Doubles

Objective: To teach fundamentals of baserunning and conditioning.

Description: Half the team stands at second base and the other half stands at home plate. On command from the coach, the runner at the plate takes off and runs a double. As soon as that runner crosses second base, the runner at second base (from the other team) starts from a position in the baseline and takes off for home plate.

Coaching point:

- This is another great drill for conditioning, but runners should also work on fundamentals.

Drill #3: Situations

Objective: To help runners work on the decision-making process along with baserunning.

Description: A group of runners starts at second base and another group starts at third base. There should be a coach at third and a coach hitting at the plate. A third player or coach tosses the ball to a coach/hitter who is skilled enough to place long fly balls or ground balls. A runner at second base and a runner at third base both react to each hit. On fly balls, the runners should retreat to their bases and advance on command from the coach. On ground balls the runner at third base should automatically try to score. The runner at second base should stay at second base on balls hit to the left side of the field, and try to advance to third on balls hit up the middle or to the right side of the field. After completing their task, the runner at second base should get in line at third base, while the runner at third base should jog to second base after crossing home plate.

Coaching point:

- The coach should pay attention to good and bad running decisions, as well as players running at full-speed.

Drill #4: Get-Back Drill

Objective: To teach runners to run at full-speed into third base until they are stopped by the coach.

Description: All the runners start at second base. On command from the coach, runners take off for third base at full-speed, assuming they are going to score. The coach stands down the line from third base and will either direct the runners to stop and return to third base or continue on to home plate. The runners should not slow down when making the turn at third base. They will have to stop immediately and retreat to third base as so directed by the coach.

Coaching point:

- This is a fun drill that makes a strong point for not slowing down until directed to by the coach. Many runs have been lost because a runner did not run hard through third base.

Drill #5: Situation—Bunting

Objective: To teach baserunners to quickly identify good and bad bunts and react accordingly.

Description: The team should be split up between all three bases. A player or coach stands in front of home plate and throws balls to a coach standing in the batter's box. All pitches should be bunted. The coach intentionally pops up some pitches, hits others for line drives, and produces some good bunts. The first runner at each base should take a lead-off when the toss is made and react to the situation. If there is a good bunt, the runners should advance to the next base. If the ball is popped-up, they should retreat. If the ball is hit in-between a good bunt and a pop-up, the runners should hold their ground and make the proper adjustment.

Coaching point:

- This drill helps runners develop quick reactions to bunting situations and an understanding for the importance of reading how good or how bad a bunt is placed.

Drill #6: Chase

Objective: Mostly serves as a conditioning drill, but it also teaches good running skills.

Description: A runner is placed at each base along with a runner placed halfway between each base. On command from the coach, all the runners start running around the bases. If runners can catch the people in front of them, they can drop out of the drill.

Coaching points:

- This drill serves as a great motivator, but the harder, faster runners will obviously be getting the least amount of work.

- This drill still works best with evenly-matched runners and is popular with young players.

Drill #7: Situations

Objective: To combine baserunning and decision-making.

Description: Players should be placed in the outfield to shag fly balls, and a couple of players should be placed at home plate to hit. Five runners start at first base, and a coach pitches (overhand or underhand) on the mound. The coach calls out the situation (hit-and-run, squeeze bunt, react, etc.) and both the hitter and the first runner at first base should respond. Both players have a task. The runner must take the lead-off on the pitch and then react to each hit or bunt.

Coaching point:

- This drill works best if there is a second coach standing behind first base to give constant input to the runner.

Drill #8: Situations—Sliding

Objective: To work on running and sliding in a game situation.

Description: The defense should be set with two shortstops, two third basemen, two catchers and someone who can throw strikes as the pitcher. The defense is working on defending against a steal at third. The coach at the plate stands with a bat, and on each pitch the coach either presents the bat as if to bunt (meaning the shortstop takes the throw at third) or stands there (meaning the third baseman retreats and takes the throw). The runners lead with the pitch and then try to steal third while working on various slides.

Coaching point:

- This drill should not be run for long. It should be restricted to 5-10 slides for each player.

Drill #9: Situations—Hitting

Objective: To practice running out of the box and running correctly through or past first base, depending on the hit.

Equipment: Pitching machine on the mound and a bucket of balls.

Description: Everyone on the team starts at home plate with their bat. A coach or a player feeds the pitching machine, and, one at a time, the hitters react as if it were a hit-and-run (they hit every pitch thrown). If the hitters/runners hit a ground ball, they should run hard down the first base line and through the bag, and then return to the end of the line after retrieving their hit. If they hit a fly ball, they should arc around the bag and run hard until going about 20 feet past the bag to simulate hitting a single and looking for the opportunity to take second. These players also retrieve their ball and return to home plate.

Coaching point:

- The runners should run hard out of the box and to the correct point past first base. Runners should not be allowed to coast on fly balls, no matter if the ball is a pop-up or a long fly ball.

Drill #10: Situations—Stealing

Objective: To help runners work on their timing when leaving the base on a steal.

Description: A pitcher should throw from the mound with a catcher positioned at home plate. The rest of the team should be at first base with the coach standing behind in order to see the runner and the pitcher's motion. With each pitch the runner can work on stealing, paying attention to a legal move (leaving the base as the pitcher releases the ball), and the explosion it takes to get a good jump. Most runners tend to leave late and need a lot of work on correct timing.

Coaching points:

- The coach should give feedback to each runner on whether they left early, late or right on time.

- The coach can also film this drill so the runners can see for themselves what they are doing right and what they are doing wrong.

Baserunning Questions

1. How can a player become a better sprinter?

Like all other skills, running requires good fundamentals and lots of practice.

2. How can a player become faster?

Technique will always help runners, but there are many drills that can enhance speed, like running hills, running with weights on the ankles, and several repetitions of running quickly.

3. Why is it important for runners to hit the inside of each base?

When runners round a base and hit the outside portion of the bag, the momentum tends to send them out towards the outfield, which increases the distance they run and slows them down.

4. Base stealing is usually done by fast runners. Should slower runners work on base stealing?

Actually, more bases are stolen by smart runners than by fast runners. Runners should always look to see if they can take a base when the defense is not paying attention or an error is made. More bases can be stolen when runners are just being alert.

5. Is it better for runners to get a quick start on hits, or should they wait until they are sure where the ball is going before they leave the base?

Percentages always favor smart runners. That doesn't mean they should wait too long before making their decision, but good decisions always come first. When players automatically take off on contact, it often leads into many double-play situations.

6. How can a player learn to slide?

First, the fear element should be taken away. Players can slide on wet grass, wet plastic or soft sand. They should start from a standing position and work up to running. Fundamentals come first, but the bottom line is that good slides come from running hard.

7. On fly balls, how do players know whether to tag-up or stay out in the baseline?

Runners should know how many outs there are, and recognize where the catch is being made in relation to them. If there are two outs, they will be running no matter what. If there are less than two outs and a deep fly ball is hit, runners may be able to tag and advance to the next base. If a runners think the ball may not be caught, they may stay out in the baseline and watch where the ball is going. Runners at third base should always want to tag-up and give themselves the opportunity to score.

8. How can runners avoid running into a defensive player?

Runners don't have to avoid defensive players. Defensive players must allow baserunners a clear path to each base unless they are fielding the ball. If there is contact, the umpire can call interference and award the runner the next base. If a runner slows down to avoid contact, no interference can be called.

9. What should the runner do if the batter misses the hit-and-run sign and doesn't swing at the pitch?

The runner at first base in that situation is stealing. If the hitter misses the ball, or just doesn't swing, the runner is still stealing, and should run hard and slide.

10. Sometimes runners may not be sure when to slide and when to come into a base standing up. How do they make these decisions?

Unless they can see the play ahead of them and know for a fact that there is no play on that base, they should always slide hard. Runners should never assume anything.

CHAPTER 10

Stealing Bases

After training runners to sprint and develop their explosiveness through practice and plyometrics, that work can be put into a game. Base stealing is a combination of speed, quickness, technique, timing, aggressiveness and sliding. Even an alert runner with average speed can take advantage of certain situations.

Beating the Infield

Players develop patterns, and good players become aware of them. If a pitcher has a great change-up, it may be used in certain situations that could be a good time to steal a base. Catchers may tend to forget about runners late in the count and infielders may not always cover the bases when they should. Baserunners should always look to steal and see who they can beat.

Timing: The First Ten Feet

The steal is made or lost in the first ten feet from the base. A runner cannot leave the base until the pitcher releases the ball. But if runners wait until they see the ball being released, before initiating any movement, they will physically be behind. It takes too long for the body to react, and the advantage goes to the defense. All runners need to know when to start the steal motion.

While pitchers are warming up, runners should be at first base timing out their first movement. A coach should stand behind the runner in order to see the pitcher's release and the runner's release. Filming from that angle is also helpful.

Runners should key on the pitcher's downward swing and find a point at which to start the steal. Some runners react a lot slower than others and need to start the steal sooner. It is important to remember that just because a runner begins movement with the upper body, it does not mean the foot has been pulled from the base. This kind of timing requires much practice throughout the year, but it is essential if a player want to successfully steal bases.

Teaching the Steal

Because the steal is made or broken in the first ten steps, the commitment to teaching that kind of quickness and explosiveness is necessary. The following discussion comes from the perspective of a controlled lead, where the runner starts off facing home plate.

The Feet
Some athletes prefer to take a step with their lead foot, while others prefer to pivot. This is nothing more than a personal preference. Some players like to initiate some weight shift, and picking up the foot will do that. There is no real drill for this factor, but the runner should know the options and recognize how far apart the feet need to be at the start of the steal.

A runner with a controlled lead.

The Right Arm
As soon as the runner has made the decision to steal, the right elbow should be driven back hard, while opening up the right shoulder and

turning the body so it is facing second base. This should be a quick and aggressive move to get the body in position to start driving to second base. Repetitions of this start are all that is needed for the runner to learn this technique.

From a controlled lead, this is the runner's first step when attempting to steal a base.

On the second step the runner looks in to home plate to see if the hitter made contact with the ball.

Driving to the Base

Once the body is turned to second base, the arms and legs need to immediately start pumping hard. There should be rapid movements of the feet off the ground, with high knee movement and the arms driving back and forth to propel the body forward. With most runners, the arms are the weakest areas. The runner does not want to stand up right away, but rather ease the body up just as a sprinter does out of the blocks. The head should be relaxed and the eyes turned into the next base.

Sliding

As soon as runners approach the base, they should notice what infielder is taking the throw. At this time runners decide which slide to utilize and where to slide. Even if the ball beats runners to the base, they can still steal the base with a good slide away from the tag.

Conclusion on Training

Most of the drills involve breaking down the skill and doing several repetitions to emphasize speed. Any time a coach can add resistance (such as using the harness or running in sand) it will build speed. Races between athletes always creates more speed. It also helps to time the runners.

Stealing Third Base

Many times, stealing third base is easier than stealing second. Runners need to be aware of where the shortstop and the third baseman are positioned. They should also watch to see how alert the pitcher and the catcher are. Coaches will often give their best runners a green light to steal third base whenever they can catch the defense off-guard.

The Delay Steal

The delay steal is used often in situations where there are runners on first and third, but it is also a good tool for a smart baserunner who is given more freedom by the coach. Runners need to have a good lead without drawing attention to themselves. If runners see that the infielders are not covering the base, or the pitcher or catcher are not alert, they are ready to steal.

Stealing home is a rare event, but it can be a backbreaker for the opposition if it can be pulled off successfully. The runner at third needs to have a great lead and be able to make a quick decision if the pitcher or catcher make a mistake. In the delay steal it is important to remember that it starts from a more up-right position. The delay steal needs to be practiced as much as regular steals because it is unique.

CHAPTER 11

Sliding

The Head-First Slide

The head-first slide is the fastest and most controlled slide. It is also the most dangerous. The slide should be taught, but it should be up to the baserunner to use it.

As runners approach the base in the head-first slide, they should drop their head and shoulders, push-off with one leg and land on their stomach, abdomen and thighs. The hands and the arms should be extended toward the base, and runners should bend at the knees to prevent them from dragging their feet. The head should be back to prevent the chin from coming in contact with the ground. Runners will glide over the ground, and their hands should reach out for the base and not be under the body. Runners should also remember to run and execute at full-speed.

1. The players should run hard.

2. The hips and shoulders drop.

3. The runners should dive out for the base.

4. The head should be back and the hands should be reaching out.

The Bent Leg Slide

This slide begins 10-15 feet from the base. Runners should drop their hips and shoot either leg out toward the base, and bend the opposite leg under the knee to form an upside down figure four. Runners will first glide over the ground, and, when on the ground, they should stay as flat as possible, keeping the head, arms and hands off the ground. The chin should be tucked lightly to the chest to protect the head. The extended foot should be 6-8 inches off the ground to prevent it from jamming into the base. Runners should slide into the base with the extended heel moving across the base, and the shin of the bent leg coming into contact with the base.

1. The player runs hard.

2. The hips are dropped and either leg is extended toward the bars.

3. The opposite leg is bent under the knee of the extended leg.

4. The head, arms and hands are kept off the ground, with the runner staying as flat as possible. The extended foot should be six to eight inches in the air.

The Pop-Up Slide

This slide starts the same way as the bent leg slide. On this slide the left leg must always be bent to assure that the runner will pop up in a position to move to the next base. The force generated by the bent leg contacting the base will bring the runner up with the body perpendicular to the ground. Runners will pop up over the base by planting their right foot on the far side of the bag and pushing off with the left foot to take off for the next base if necessary.

The Hook Slide
The hook slide is used to slide away from the ball and minimize the area to be tagged. It is an advanced slide and should only be taught to older players who are good sliders.

When approaching the base, runners should slightly angle the running pattern toward the infield side of the base, with the slide beginning 8-10 feet away from the base. In one continuous motion, the right leg should be planted, with the left leg thrown toward the infield and the hips being dropped. Runners should glide over the top of the ground. The trailing leg should be straightened out and reach for the bag. The base should be contacted with the top third of the right foot as runners continue the slide past the base to create the hook.

Teaching Techniques
Since there is a certain fear element to deal with, it is important to devise ways to make sliding fun and easy. Some very young players, though, may not be able to slide because of their fear, and should never be forced until they are ready.

Breaking Down the Skills
The biggest element of fear comes from running at full-speed and launching the body through the air. The larger or taller the player is, the more fear that may be involved. That is why the skills should be broken down to connect the transition between running and sliding.

Coaches can start with a sand pit or wet grass so the surface will be soft. For the bent leg slide (refer to diagram 11-3), players should squat down and place their left hand on the ground to support the body weight. The players should then throw out their legs and try to land on their behind first and then their back. This gives players an idea of the movement required to accomplish the slide. For the head-first slide (refer to diagram 11-4), the players should squat down like a frog and then dive out in front, just like they were performing a volleyball dive.

Bent leg slide

A. The player starts by squatting down and placing the left hand on the ground to support the body weight.

B. The player then throws out her leg and tries to land on her behind first, and then her back.

Head-first slide

A. The player squats down like a frog.

B. The player then dives as if performing a volleyball dive.

Once the players have the right idea on how to throw their bodies, they need to learn to run at full-speed so they can launch their bodies out toward the bag, instead of jumping up. If runners hesitate and then jump up, they will land hard on the ground. Players need to remember that it is a slide, not a jump.

In going full-speed, the best tools to use are a sand pit or a slip-and-slide (refer to diagram 11-5). Both tools will provide a soft surface. The slick wet plastic will aid runners in their slide. The more that athletes can lose their fear of throwing their body through the air, the better at sliding they will become. To help them relate to the base, coaches should be sure to have a safe base by the side of the plastic so the sliders can aim for it.

Players can practice sliding in a sand pit.

A slip-n-slide can be used to help learn how to slide.

CHAPTER 12

Offensive Strategy and How to Attack the Defense

An offensive philosophy aims to attack the defense. Whatever style a coach chooses, it should be aimed at beating the defense. Coaches need to evaluate their talent, and that will change from year to year. The basic philosophy of execution, aggression and awareness will always stay the same, but the players will dictate what adjustments have to be made.

Factors a coach needs to look for when developing an offensive strategy are individual and team speed, hitters who hit for a high average, hitters who hit for power, bunting ability (this is the only constant because it can be taught), contact hitters and the type of pitching staff on the team and team defense.

Tools used in applying the philosophy include bunting (sacrifice, drag, slap, bunt-and-run, squeeze), stealing (straight, delay, double steal), and the hit-and-run.

Questions to answer about the players include who are the best bunters (sacrifice, drag, slap), who are the best hitters (for high average, runs batted in, contact), and who are the best baserunners (speed and smarts).

Making the Line-Up

Factors to Consider About Each Position in the Batting Order

1. Speed, great on-base percentage, knows the strike zone, good baserunner
2. Speed, good bunter, knows the strike zone, good bat control
3. Best hitter on the team, hits for high average, good at driving in runs, power
4. Power, good at driving in runs, good batting average
5. Same as the fourth batter, but not as consistent of a hitter
6. Either good speed and contact like the second hitter, or good at driving in runs but has a low batting average
7-9. Most inconsistent hitters, possibly clutch hitters or good bunters; a hitter with a high batting average but a low total of runs batted in is ideal for the 8th position.

Sample Line-Ups

Normal Line-Up

1. Speed
2. Speed
3. Best hitter
4. Power-RBIs
5. Power-RBIs
6. RBIs or speed
7. Good bunter
8. Best hitter in bottom half of line-up
9. Good bunter, has bat control

Speed Line-Up

1. Speed
2. Speed
3. Speed
4. Hitter
5. Hitter
6. Hitter
7. Hitter
8. Speed
9. Speed

Strategy

When to Bunt or Steal

1. Speed of the baserunner—The faster the runner is, the higher the percentage of success in steals. With slower runners, coaches should go more with sacrifice or drag bunts and bunt-and-run calls.

2. Defensive alignment—If the defense is playing tight at the corners, it takes away sacrifice bunts. That leaves slaps, steals and hit-and-run options.

3. Strength of catcher's arm—If the pitcher's speed and the catcher's arm are faster than the runner, it eliminates stealing unless those two players are not alert.

4. Infield awareness—From pitch to pitch, a defense will change, and so will their discipline. Coaches should check to see how the defense is reacting to determine the best situations for each play.

5. Number of outs (and what player is on-deck)—The number of outs is important because it will dictate whether the coach will have one or two chances to score a run after moving a runner to second base. If there is a good bunter at the plate, followed by a good hitter, the bunt can help. But if the situation is reversed, coaches don't want to lose their better hitters by having them bunt. The number of outs obviously figures in that call. In a different situation, if there is a runner at first base and a good hitter at the plate with two outs, that could be a good time to call for a steal to give the hitter the opportunity to drive in a run. If the runner is out trying the steal, the coach still starts off the next inning with a good hitter at the plate.

When to Utilize the Hit-and-Run

1. Speed of the baserunner—This comes into play with both a fast and a slow baserunner. With speed, this play enables the runner to steal, possibly advance two bases, or keep out of a double-play. It also allows the hitter to concentrate on just hitting the ball. Also, with the shortstop leaving position to cover the steal, it may open a hole in the infield through which the hitter can place the ball. With a slow runner on base, it keeps the team out of a double-play, and usually guarantees a runner moving into scoring position.

2. Defensive alignment—Many times a hit-and-run is a good call in typical bunting situations. It can catch the first and third basemen off-guard and may force an error. Because of defensive positioning, it may even open more holes for hitting and provide a better opportunity for the steal.

3. Type of hitter at the plate—The hitter should have good bat control and make consistent contact. A big swinger who strikes out a lot is not desirable for the hit-and-run. Contact by the hitter is the most important factor.

4. Number of outs—One reason for this play is to advance a runner into scoring position, so it would be used with less than two outs. If the coach is trying to generate some runs, or create excitement, the outs don't matter. A coach may also use this play because the weak part of the batting order is coming up, and this may be the last opportunity to score.

5. Mental frame of the hitter—Sometimes when a hitter becomes tentative, takes too many strikes or is in a batting slump, the hit-and-run frees the hitter from all decisions except to find the ball and hit it hard. It can be called whether or not there is a baserunner.

Studying and Experimenting
There is no point in training athletes if the coach is not going to make a commitment to use those skills during the games. For any coach, calling offensive plays is a learning experience, and more learning comes with more experimenting.

Coaches should study their players and the opponents to decide how to attack the defense. These plays should be tried in normal practice situations, not just in games. Coaches should look at how their team reacts, both offensively and defensively.

Finally, creativity is essential. The worst thing an offense can be is predictable.

AUTHORS

Susan Craig has been the head coach of the New Mexico softball program for over 20 years. She has led the Lobos to three conference championships and three national post-season appearances during her tenure.

Craig has compiled over 400 victories and has been named Conference Coach of the Year three times. Her primary responsibility is handling the pitching staff.

A member of the NCAA National Softball Committee, and the first president of the National Softball Coaches Association, Craig and co-head coach Ken Johnson co-authored *The Softball Handbook*. That book is used extensively throughout the United States and many English-speaking countries as a standard tool for understanding the sport of softball.

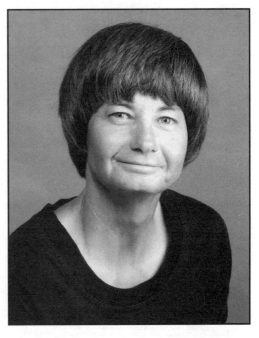

Craig's softball program at New Mexico has produced four All-Americans, 35 All-Region players and over 60 All-Conference athletes.

Susan Craig played major ASA fast-pitch softball, and was named to the All-Regional team as a second baseman three times.

Ken Johnson served as an assistant to Susan Craig for five years before being elevated to head coach status in 1984. Johnson is the Lobos' fundamentals coach, and is the primary signal caller for the New Mexico offense.

Johnson is a New Mexico graduate and a former member of the Lobo baseball team. As a member of the New Mexico baseball team, he set a team record for stolen bases and triples in a single season. He was also a long-standing NCAA record holder for most stolen bases in a single game.

Prior to joining the Lobo softball program, Johnson taught and coached in the Albuquerque Public Schools system. He has over 30 years of playing and coaching experience to his credit.

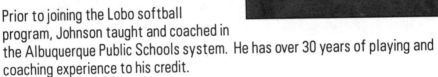

As a shortstop on the National Electric Chiefs in Chicago, Johnson contributed to two AABC national championships. He taught and coached at the high school level for seven years before joining the New Mexico staff in 1979.